THE AUDACITY OF THE BLOOD OF JESUS

"And they overcame him by the blood of the Lamb, and by the word of their testimony; and they loved not their lives unto the death."

Rev12:11

The Audacity of the Blood of Jesus

COPYRIGHT 2018 BY Franklin N Abazie
ISBN: 978:0-9966-263-30

All right reserved. This book or any portion thereof may not be reproduced or used in any manner whatsoever without the express written permission of the publisher, except for the use of brief quotations in a book review. All Bible quotes are from King James Version and others as noted.

Published by: F N ABAZIE PUBLISHING HOUSE---
a.k.a,
Empowerment Bookstore:

That I may publish with the voice of thanksgiving and tell of all thy wondrous works. **Psalms26:7**

To order additional copies, wholesales or booking: Call the Church office (973-372-7518)
or Empowerment Bookstore Hotline 973-393-8518
Worship address:
343 Sanford Avenue Newark New Jersey 07106
Administrative Head Office address:
33 Schley Street Newark New Jersey 07112
Email:pastorfranknto@yahoo.com
Website www.fnabaziehealingministries.org
Publishing House: www.fnabaziepublishinghouse.org

This book is a production of F N Abazie Publishing House.

A publication Arms of Miracle of God Ministries 2018
First Edition

CONTENTS

THE MANDATE OF THE COMMISSION...........iv

ARMS OF THE COMMISSION............................v

INTRODUCTION..viii

CHAPTER 1

1. The Overcoming Power in the blood of Jesus..51

CHAPTER 2

2. The Testimonial Power in the blood of Jesus....63

CHAPTER 3

3. Prayer of Salvation..82

CHAPTER 4

4. About the Author...92

THE MANDATE OF THE COMMISSION

"THE MOMENT IS DUE TO IMPACT YOUR WORLD THROUGH THE REVIVAL OF THE HEALING & MIRACLE MINISTRY OF JESUS CHRIST OF NAZARETH.

I AM SENDING YOU TO RESTORE HEALTH UNTO THEE AND I WILL HEAL THEE OF THY WOUNDS, SAID THE LORD OF HOST."

ARMS OF THE COMMISSION

1) F N Abazie Ministries-Miracle of God Ministries (Miracle Chapel Intl)

2) F N Abazie TV Ministries: Global Television Ministry Outreach.

3) F N Abazie Radio Ministries: Radio Broadcasting Outreach.

4) F N Abazie Publishing House: Book Publication.

5) F N Abazie Bible School: also called Word of Healing Bible School (W.O.H.B.S)

6) F N Abazie Evangelistic Ass: Miracle of God Ministries: Global Crusade

7) Empowerment Bookstore: Book distribution.

8) F N Abazie Helping Hands: Meeting the help of the needy world wide

9) F N Abazie Disaster Recovery Mission: Global Disaster Recovery.

10) F N Abazie Prison Ministry: Prison Ministry for all convicts "Second chance"

Some of our ministry arms are waiting the appointed time to commence

FAVOR CONFESSION

Father thank you for making me righteous and accepted through the blood of Jesus Christ. Because of that, I am blessed and highly favored by God. I am the subject of your affection. Your favor surrounds me as a shield, and the first thing that people see around me is your favored shield.

Thank you that I have favor with you and man today. All day long people go out of their way to bless me and help me. I have favor with everyone that I deal with today. Doors that were once closed are now opened for me. I receive preferential treatment, and I have special privileges, I am Gods favored child.

No good thing will he withhold from me. Because of Gods favor my enemies cannot triumph over my life. I have supernatural increase and promotion. I declare restoration to everything that the devil has stolen from my life. I have honor in the midst of my adversaries and an increase in assets, especially in real estate and expansion of territories.

Because I am highly favored by God, I experience great victories, supernatural turnarounds, and miraculous breakthrough in the midst of great impossibilities. I receive recognition, prominence, and honor. Petitions are granted to me even by ungodly authorities. Policies, rules, regulations, and laws are changed and reverse on my behalf.

I win battles that I don't even have to fight, because God fights them for me. This is the day, the set time and the designated moment for me to experience the free favor of God, that profusely and lavishly abound on my behalf in Jesus name. Amen.

INTRODUCTION

"And they overcame him by the blood of the Lamb, and by the word of their testimony; and they loved not their lives unto the death." **Rev12:11**

I may never meet with you in person. However, I am glad to meet with you here. I love the power of books in print. We are told but the word of God is not bound. In this small book, you will be excited to know more about the blood of Jesus. The blood of Jesus is our last card.

"For I will pass through the land of Egypt this night, and will smite all the firstborn in the land of Egypt, both man and beast; and against all the gods of Egypt I will execute judgment: I am the Lord." **Exodus12:12**

"And the blood shall be to you for a token upon the houses where ye are: and when I see the blood, I will pass over you, and the plague shall not be upon you to destroy you, when I smite the land of Egypt." **Exodus12:13.**

We were told ..

> *"No weapon that is formed against thee shall prosper; and every tongue that shall rise against thee in judgment thou shalt condemn. ..."*

We must take advantage of the blood of Jesus Christ by appropriating it in the respective area of our lives.

Ignorant of the power in the blood of Jesus makes us vulnerable to wiles of the devil. This book is a book of encouragement, boldness, and victory against the wiles and schemes of the devil. Therefore put aside all your secular theories and come with me as revealed by the Holy Spirit the hidden powers in the blood of Jesus Christ.

Happy Reading!

HIS DESTINY WAS THE CROSS….

HIS PURPOSE WAS LOVE…..

HIS REASON WAS YOU….

"But if we walk in the light, as he is in the light, we have fellowship one with another, and the blood of Jesus Christ his Son cleanseth us from all sin."

1 John 1:7

"For this is my blood of the new testament, which is shed for many for the remission of sins."

Matthew 26:28

"And almost all things are by the law purged with blood; and without shedding of blood is no remission."

Hebrews 9:22

"Neither by the blood of goats and calves, but by his own blood he entered in once into the holy place, having obtained eternal redemption for us."

Hebrews 9:12

" And the blood shall be to you for a token upon the houses where ye are: and when I see the blood, I will pass over you, and the plague shall not be upon you to destroy [you], when I smite the land of Egypt."

Exodus 12:13

"And from Jesus Christ, [who is] the faithful witness, [and] the first begotten of the dead, and the prince of the kings of the earth. Unto him that loved us, and washed us from our sins in his own blood."

Rev1:5

"And they overcame him by the blood of the Lamb, and by the word of their testimony; and they loved not their lives unto the death."

Revelation 12:11

"Now the God of peace, that brought again from the dead our Lord Jesus, that great shepherd of the sheep, through the blood of the everlasting covenant."

Hebrews 13:20

"How much more shall the blood of Christ, who through the eternal Spirit offered himself without spot to God, purge your conscience from dead works to serve the living God?"

Hebrews 9:14

"For it is not possible that the blood of bulls and of goats should take away sins."

Hebrews 10:4

"Take heed therefore unto yourselves, and to all the flock, over the which the Holy Ghost hath made you overseers, to feed the church of God, which he hath purchased with his own blood."

Acts 20:28

"For the life of the flesh is in the blood: and I have given it to you upon the altar to make an atonement for your souls: for it is the blood that maketh an atonement for the soul."

Leviticus 17:11

"Of how much sorer punishment, suppose ye, shall he be thought worthy, who hath trodden under foot the Son of God, and hath counted the blood of the covenant, wherewith he was sanctified, an unholy thing, and hath done despite unto the Spirit of grace?"

Hebrews 10:29

"In whom we have redemption through his blood, even the forgiveness of sins:"

Col1:14

"And he said, What hast thou done? the voice of thy brother's blood crieth unto me from the ground."

Genesis 4:10

"But flesh with the life thereof, which is the blood thereof, shall ye not eat."

Genesis 9:4

"And to Jesus the mediator of the new covenant, and to the blood of sprinkling, that speaketh better things than that of Abel."

Hebrews 12:24

"Having therefore, brethren, boldness to enter into the holiest by the blood of Jesus."

Hebrews 10:19-22

"Who is he that overcometh the world, but he that believeth that Jesus is the Son of God?"

1 John 5:5-8

The Blood of Jesus Prayer Points

Blood of Jesus deliver me by fire in the Name of Jesus.

I command all my blessings confiscated by rulers of darkness to be released, in the Name of Jesus.

I cut myself off from every territorial spirit, in the Name of Jesus.

I command all demonic reverse gears installed to hinder my progress to be roasted, in the Name of Jesus.

Lord Jesus, bear all my physical and spiritual burdens now, in the Name of Jesus.

Every power stealing my virtues die, in the Name of Jesus.

Every power in the heavenlies, on earth and in the seas hindering the angel of my blessings, die, in the Name of Jesus.

Any power diverting the blessings of God away from me, your time is up, die now, in the Name of Jesus.

By the Blood of Jesus, every owner of evil load, carry your load in the Name of Jesus.

Blood of Jesus, pursue my pursuers in the Name of Jesus.

Blood of Jesus, arise and fight my battles, in the Name of Jesus.

Blood of Jesus, pursue poverty out of my life, in the Name of Jesus.

Every power assigned to follow me, to destroy me, die in the Name of Jesus.- Therefore, let our enemies be delivered into the hands of their enemies in Jesus name!

It is written, *"You shall be for fuel of fire; your blood shall be in the midst of the land. You shall not be remembered, for I the Lord have spoken"* **(Ezekiel. 21:32)**

Therefore, let all our spiritual enemies become fuel for divine fire in Jesus name!

It is written; *then they will know that I am the Lord, when I have set a fire in Egypt and all her helpers are destroyed* **(Ezekiel. 30:8)**

Therefore, O Lord, let all the helpers of our enemies be destroyed in the name of Jesus.

It is written; *and the people to whom they prophesy shall be cast out in the streets of Jerusalem because of the famine and the sword; they will have no one to bury them – them nor their wives, their sons nor their daughters – for I will pour their wickedness on them* **(Jer. 14:16)**.

Therefore, O Lord, pour the wickedness of those who seek to destroy us upon their own heads in the name of Jesus!

It is written; *call together the archers against Babylon. All you who bend the bow encamp against it all around; let none of them escape. Repay her according to her work; According to all she has done, do to her; for she has been poured against the Lord, against the Holy one of Israel* **(Jer. 50:29)**.

Therefore, let all the hosts of the Lord turn against our spiritual enemies in Jesus name!

It is written; *let God arise, let His enemies be scattered; let those also who hate him flee before him* **(Psalms. 68:1)**.

Therefore, O God, arise and let all your enemies in our lives be scattered in Jesus name!

It is written; *and He that searches the hearts knows what the mind of the spirit is, because He makes intercession for the saints according to the will of God* **(Romans 8:27)**

Therefore, the intercessory prayers of Jesus, who is seated on the right hand of the throne of God, will not be in vain over our lives, in the name of Jesus.

It is written; *the Lord is your keeper; the Lord is the shade at your right hand. The sun shall not strike you by day, nor the moon by night. The Lord shall preserve you from all evil; He shall preserve your soul. The Lord shall preserve our going out and our coming in from this time forth, and even forevermore* **(Psalms. 121:5-8)**

Therefore, O Lord, spread your covering of fire and the blood of Jesus over us and our loved ones, in the name of Jesus.

It is written; *rejoice always, pray without ceasing, in everything give thanks; for this is the will of God in Christ Jesus for you* (**1 Thess. 5:16:18**).

Therefore, we thank you Father, for raising a spiritual shield over our loved ones and us. Thank you for giving us the heart for appreciating everything you are doing for us. Thank you for filling our hearts and our home with joy and peace that surpasses all understanding. Blessed be your name for all the answers to our prayers in the name of Jesus!

You are holy, holy, Lord God Almighty, who was and is and is to come, Amen!

O Lord, let our season of divine intervention appear in the name of Jesus!

O you gates in the heavenlies standing against our destiny, lift up your heads in the name of Jesus!

O you gates in the waters standing against our destiny, lift up your heads in the name of Jesus!

O you gates in the earth standing against our destiny, lift up your heads in the name of Jesus!

O you gates under the earth standing against our destiny, lift up your heads in the name of Jesus!

O God, arise and destroy every gate keeper assigned against our lives in the name of Jesus!

We break the backbone of every spirit of scarcity in our lives in the name of Jesus!

O Lord anoint our eyes to see divine opportunities in the name of Jesus!

Lord let every blindness to the treasures of our lives be cleared in the name of Jesus!

Let our divine helpers appear in the name of Jesus!

We declare, O Lord that will overcome obstacles and defeat every enemy, in Jesus name!

We declare, O Lord that every blessing and promise that you put in our hearts will come to pass because this is our time for favor, in Jesus name!

We declare, O Lord that this is a new season of increase in our lives. We speak health, wisdom, creativity, divine connections, and supernatural opportunities. They are coming our way, in Jesus name!

We declare, O Lord that we choose faith over fear. We are victorious in faith, in Jesus name!

We declare, O Lord that that we are not just surviving, this is our time to thrive in prosperity, in Jesus name!

We declare, O Lord that we will believe that we have received in the spirit even though we do not see anything happening in the flesh, in Jesus name!

We declare, O Lord that our rewards are being transferred to us because we remain in faith, in Jesus name!

We declare, O Lord that doubt will not ruin our optimistic spirit, in Jesus name!

We declare, O Lord that we are prisoners of hope and get up every morning expecting your favor, in Jesus name!

We declare, O Lord that you will do amazing things in our lives, in Jesus name!

We declare, O Lord that we are closer to your abundant blessing than we think, our time has come, your promises will come to pass, in Jesus name!

We declare, O Lord that we will stay in an attitude of faith and expectation, in Jesus name!

We declare, O Lord that we are not worried, we know that you are our vindicator. It may seem to be taking a long time, but we will reap in due season if trust in you Lord, in Jesus name!

We declare, O Lord that you know the secret petitions our heart and we believe that they will come to fulfilment, in Jesus name!

We declare, O Lord that you will open new doors for us, in Jesus name!

We declare, O Lord that we will see your goodness, in Jesus name!

We declare, O Lord that this is our time to believe because favor is coming our way, in Jesus name!

We declare, O Lord that you have paved the way to abundant prosperity for us, prosperity more than we can every dream of or imagine, for your sake, in Jesus name!

We declare, O Lord that in your eyes our future is extremely bright, in Jesus name!

We declare, O Lord that we will rise higher and higher and see more of your favor and blessings and we will live the prosperous life you have in store for us, in Jesus name!

We declare, O Lord that we may have a lot of turmoil, but we know that everything is going to be alright, in Jesus name!

We declare, O Lord that we have faith because we have put you first, in Jesus name!

We thank you, O Lord that our set time for favor is here, in Jesus name!

We declare, O Lord that our hour of deliverance has come, in Jesus name!

We declare, O Lord that there is no limit to what we can do, in Jesus name!

We declare, O Lord that there is no obstacle we cannot overcome, in Jesus name!

We declare, O Lord that that we have seen your accomplishments and they are good, in Jesus name!

We declare, O Lord that there is no challenge that is too great for us because you are with us, in Jesus name!

We declare, O Lord that you always succeed, in Jesus name!

We declare, O Lord that there is no financial difficulty or situation in our lives that is too great for you to resolve, in Jesus name!

We declare, O Lord that you are our Father Jehovah Jireh and that you own everything and you are our provider, in Jesus name!

We declare, O Lord that your promises declare that we are destined to live a victorious life, in Jesus name!

We declare, O Lord that we are your children, in Jesus name!

We declare, O Lord that the seeds of increase, success, and promotion are taking a new root; your favor will spring forth in our lives in a great way; we will see new seasons of blessings and new seasons of your favor. It's our time to have abundant faith, in Jesus name!

O Lord, it is written; according to your faith, it will be done unto you. Ps. 2:8 says *"ask me and I will give you the nations as your inheritance."*

Therefore, we ask you Lord to fulfil our highest hopes and dreams, in Jesus name!

We ask you this day, O Lord to give us our abundant blessing now, in Jesus name!

We dare to exercise our faith by asking you O Lord so that we may receive indeed, in Jesus name!

We thank you O Lord that for encouraging our faith, in Jesus name!

We declare, O Lord that this is our time for favor, in Jesus name!

We declare, O Lord that this is our time to prosper abundantly, in Jesus name!

We declare, O Lord that this is our time to have instant answers to prayer, in Jesus name!

We declare, O Lord that this is our time to ask and receive, in Jesus name!

We declare, O Lord that this is our time to thank you and testify for answered prayer, in Jesus name!

We declare, O Lord that we are blessed and that goodness and mercy are following us right now, in Jesus name!

We declare, O Lord that you favor is surrounding us like a shield – you prosper us even in the desert, in Jesus name!

We declare, O Lord that you have great things for us in the spirit and that you have already released favor into our prayers, in Jesus name!

We declare, O Lord that you are a great and Holy God, in Jesus name!

It is written; *delight yourself in the Lord and he will give you the desires of your heart* **(Ps 37:4)**.

We therefore declare, O Lord that we delight in you because you are our Father God and because we are your children you have made us the head and not the tail.

We declare, O Lord that because we are your children, we are more than conquerors, in Jesus name!

We declare, O Lord that we are blessed and you supply all our needs. We have more than enough, in Jesus name!

We declare, O Lord that we have abundant favor indeed, in Jesus name!

We declare, O Lord that we are filled indeed with the presence of the Holy Spirit, in Jesus name!

We declare, O Lord that we have abundant faith indeed, in Jesus name!

We declare, O Lord that you have answered our prayers, in Jesus name!

We declare, O Lord that our debts are all paid up, in Jesus name!

We declare, O Lord that we are healthy, in Jesus name!

We declare, O Lord that we have no lack and that we have more than enough, in Jesus name!

We declare, O Lord that we are extremely blessed so much that we can bless your kingdom, in Jesus name!

We declare, O Lord that you have answered our prayers, in Jesus name!

We declare, O Lord that our debts are all paid up, in Jesus name!

We declare, O Lord that we are healthy, in Jesus name!

We declare, O Lord that we have no lack and that we have more than enough, in Jesus name!

We declare, O Lord that we are extremely blessed so much that we can bless your kingdom, in Jesus name!

We declare, O Lord that we are extremely blessed so much that we can bless others, in Jesus name!

We declare, O Lord that we have entered into an anointing of ease, in Jesus name!

We declare, O Lord that for every opportunity we have missed, every chance we've blown, you will turn the clock and bring bigger and better things across our path, in Jesus name!

We declare, O Lord that we will not settle for less than your best, in Jesus name!

Please restore the time that we have lost, O Lord that, in Jesus name!

Restore our victories, O Lord, in Jesus name!

Restore our lost joy, lost peace, lost health, lost insight, lost faith, lost dedication, and desire to please you, we declare, O Lord in Jesus name!

We declare, O Lord that you use what was meant for our harm to our advantage, in Jesus name!

We declare, O Lord that you are a faithful God, in Jesus name!

We declare, O Lord that you will blossom our lives in ways that we can never imagine, in Jesus name!

We know, O Lord that you will bless us abundantly, in Jesus name!

We know, O Lord that you will provide divine connections, in Jesus name!

We declare, O Lord that we are not suffering – we are blessed, in Jesus name!

We declare, O Lord that our difficulties will give way to new growth, new opportunities, and new vision, in Jesus name!

O Lord let us see your blessing bloom in our lives in ways we would never dreamt possible, in Jesus name!

We declare, O Lord that we will stay in faith, so that what was meant to stop us will not be a stumbling block but a stepping stone taking us to a higher level, in Jesus name!

We declare, O Lord that we are not ordinary, but we are children of the most high God, in Jesus name!

We declare, O Lord that we created to rise above problems, in Jesus name!

We declare victory over strife O Lord, in Jesus name!

We declare, O Lord that no weapon formed against us shall prosper, in Jesus name!

We declare, O Lord that we are healthy and that no sickness shall live in us, in Jesus name!

We declare, O Lord that triumph is our birthright, in Jesus name!

We declare, O Lord that our setbacks are simply setups for greater comebacks that will place us to be better than we were before, in Jesus name!

We declare, O Lord that with you all things are possible, in Jesus name!

We declare, O Lord that we are in agreement with you. We know you have supernatural favor in store for us. You have supernatural opportunities, supernatural healing, and supernatural restoration, in Jesus name!

We declare, O Lord that you want to do unusual things in our lives, in Jesus name!

We declare, O Lord that in faith, we have expectation deep in our spirits, in Jesus name!

We declare, O Lord that this will not be a survival year but a supernatural year in which you will abundantly come through for us, in Jesus name!

We believe, O Lord that you have come through for us, in Jesus name!

We declare, O Lord that because we hope in you, we will not be put to shame, in Jesus name!

We declare, O Lord that your word is right and true, you are faithful in all you do, in Jesus name!

We declare, O Lord that you are our refuge and strength, an ever present helper, in Jesus name!

We declare, O Lord that we will cast our cares on you and you will sustain us, you will never let the righteous fall, in Jesus name!

We declare, O Lord that you are the strength of our hearts and our portion forever, in Jesus name!

We declare, O Lord that you are our dwelling, therefore, no harm will befall us, and no disaster will come near our tent, in Jesus name!

We declare, O Lord that you are our refuge and our fortress, in Jesus name!

We declare, O Lord that you will command your angels concerning us to guard us in all our ways, in Jesus name!

We declare, O Lord that even in darkness the light will dawn for us, in Jesus name!

We declare, O Lord that your word is eternal and stands firm in the heavens, in Jesus name!

We declare, O Lord that your faithfulness will continue throughout all generations, in Jesus name!

We declare, O Lord that you will keep us from harm; you will watch over our lives; you will watch over our coming and our going both now and for evermore, in Jesus name! (Ps. 121)

Thank you O Lord for the assurance that you are watching over us even when we sleep, in Jesus name! (Ps. 13:5-6)

We declare, O Lord that you will drive those that do evil away from us and that you will protect us from their influence, in Jesus name! (Ps. 66:1-4)

We will shout with joy to you O Lord, we will sing the glory of your name and make your praise glorious. How awesome are your deeds! So great is your power that your enemies cringe before you, in Jesus name!

We declare, O Lord that that we will give you thanks for you answered us, in Jesus name! (Ps. 118:2)

We declare, O Lord that we will praise you with all our hearts; before the gods we will sing your praise. We will bow down towards your Holy temple and will praise your name for your love and your faithfulness, for you have exalted above all things, your name and your word, in Jesus name! (Ps. 138:1-3)

AMEN.

CHAPTER 1
The Overcoming Power in the blood of Jesus

"...Unto him that loved us, and washed us from our sins in his own blood." **Rev 1:5**

As sacrifice, blood is very significant to God. That is why it is mentioned almost about seven hundred times in the bible. Peter called the blood of Jesus the "incorruptible blood" John revelator called it "the overcoming" power of the blood.

As our natural blood supplies life-giving oxygen and nutrients to every cell in our body, so does the blood of Jesus supply life, protection, and defense to every area of our spirit, soul, and body.

Physiologically speaking, if the flow of blood were to be cut off from an area of our body, that part would begin to die. Likewise, any part of our life that is cut off from the blood of Jesus is vulnerable to the wiles and schemes of the devil.

Our blood also carries away wastes and toxins from our cells. Spiritually, without the blood of Jesus, our life would be filled with filth.

Remember...

The life of the flesh is in the blood.

God shaped our body with white blood cells that fight off sickness. Any time bacteria or viruses that try to get in, our white cells attack that intruder immediately. When our natural blood is healthy, we are protected from sickness and diseases; likewise, we are protected from the wiles and schemes of the devil every time we plead the blood of Jesus Christ.

There is no trick the devil will pull on us that the overcoming blood cannot handle. We are told, *"For even Christ our passover is sacrificed for us."*

The blood of Jesus is a powerful tool in the mouth of the believer. We are told, *"And almost all things are by the law purged with blood; and without shedding of blood is no remission."* **Hebrew 9:22**

Chapter 1 - The Overcoming Power in the Blood of Jesus

Although Jesus died and took away our sins, He gave us the overcoming power through His blood.

Hear This!

"And they overcame him by the blood of the Lamb, and by the word of their testimony; and they loved not their lives unto the death." **Rev 12:11.**

Every time we apply the blood of Jesus against any opposition or uprising, it works like fire. Perhaps you do not know this, the blood of Jesus Christ is the warrant for the arrest of the devil. So to say, every time we apply the blood of Jesus, we issue a spiritual summon for the arrest of the devil.

I encourage you to take advantage of the blood of Jesus. It is free! Thank you Jesus for your precious blood. Hallelujah!

The blood of Jesus is an instrument of restoration, reconciliation, redemption, and cleansing. Every time you pray, never forget to plead the blood of Jesus Christ. Know this: the blood of Jesus will never lose its power, but it will only make a difference in our life when we apply it.

WE ARE REDEEMED BY THE BLOOD OF JESUS

The bible says *"For as much as ye know that ye were not redeemed with corruptible things, as silver and gold, from your vain conversation received by tradition from your fathers; But with the precious blood of Christ, as of a lamb without blemish and without spot:"* **1Peter1:18-19**

My bible says, *"Let the redeemed of the Lord say so, whom he hath redeemed from the hand of the enemy;"* **Psalms107:2**

You must appropriate the blood of Jesus Christ every time you pray, or every time you are in trouble.

"Who hath delivered us from the power of darkness, and hath translated us into the kingdom of his dear Son: In whom we have redemption through his blood, even the forgiveness of sins:" **Col1:13-14**.

Chapter 1 - The Overcoming Power in the Blood of Jesus

Declare this by faith in the blood of Jesus Christ right now

I cover my life with the blood of Jesus.

I cover my family with the blood of Jesus.

I cover my job with the blood of Jesus.

I plead the Blood of Jesus for my healing.

I resist you devil with the Blood of the Lamb.

I plead the blood of Jesus over my business and education.

I plead the blood of Jesus over my wife/husband.

I plead the Blood of the Lord Jesus Christ against this problem.

I cover my home with the Blood of Jesus to protect all occupants and possessions from all evil.

THE CLEANSING POWER IN THE BLOOD OF JESUS CHRIST

Are you living in sin?

The blood of Jesus is the only way out against all immoralities and unrighteousness. The word of God said If we confess our sins, he is faithful and just to forgive us our sins, and to cleanse us from all unrighteousness.

"But if we walk in the light, as he is in the light, we have fellowship one with another, and the blood of Jesus Christ his Son cleanseth us from all sin." **1John1:7**

"And almost all things are by the law purged with blood; and without shedding of blood is no remission." **Hebrews9:22**

"How much more shall the blood of Christ, who through the eternal Spirit offered himself without spot to God, purge your conscience from dead works to serve the living God?" **Hebrews9:14**

Chapter 1 - The Overcoming Power in the Blood of Jesus

We thank God, for the Blood of Jesus Christ. For without shedding of blood is no remission. I encourage you to take advantage of the cleansing Power in the blood.

Remember....

"For the life of the flesh is in the blood: and I have given it to you upon the altar to make an atonement for your souls: for it is the blood that maketh an atonement for the soul." **Leviticus 17:11**

FAITH IN THE BLOOD OF JESUS CHRIST

Do you believe in the blood of Jesus?

The Holy bible says, without faith we cannot please Him. Do you have faith in the working Power of the blood of Jesus?

"Whom God hath set forth to be a propitiation through faith in his blood, to declare his righteousness for the remission of sins that are past, through the forbearance of God;" **Romans 3:25**

We must develop genuine faith in the blood of Jesus. Apostle Paul said I do not frustrate the grace of God: for if righteousness come by the law, then Christ is dead in vain.

Our faith in the blood of Jesus Christ must be unconditional. The same way, our love for God is unconditional, our faith in Christ and in the blood of Jesus Christ must be unconditional. Never doubt if it will work, or if it will not work.

Hear this!!

"Through faith he kept the passover, and the sprinkling of blood, lest he that destroyed the firstborn should touch them." **Hebrew 11:28**

THE SPEAKING POWER IN THE BLOOD OF JESUS CHRIST.

The blood of Jesus is so powerful that it has power to cry out against molestation, discrimination, torture, fear, and torment. e.t.c. The truth is the blood of Jesus is has power to fight back our opposition

Chapter 1 - The Overcoming Power in the Blood of Jesus

"And to Jesus the mediator of the new covenant, and to the blood of sprinkling, that speaketh better things than that of Abel." **Hebrews 12:24**

"And he said, What hast thou done? the voice of thy brother's blood crieth unto me from the ground." **Genesis 4:10**

"Neither by the blood of goats and calves, but by his own blood he entered in once into the holy place, having obtained eternal redemption for us." **Hebrews 9:12**

"For it is not possible that the blood of bulls and of goats should take away sins." **Hebrews 10:4**

THE SPRINKLING POWER IN THE BLOOD OF JESUS CHRIST

"Elect according to the foreknowledge of God the Father, through sanctification of the Spirit, unto obedience and sprinkling of the blood of Jesus Christ: Grace unto you, and peace, be multiplied." **1 Peter 1:2**

And Moses took the blood, and sprinkled it on the people, and said, Behold the blood of the covenant, which the Lord hath made with you concerning all these words. **Hebrews9:22.**

I encourage you to take advantage of the sprinkling Power in the blood of Jesus.

THE IMPORTANCE OF THE BLOOD OF JESUS

THE BLOOD OF JESUS CHRIST DRAWS US CLOSER TO GOD

"But now in Christ Jesus you who once were far off have been brought near by the blood of Christ." **(Ephesians 2:13)**

CLEANSES OUR CONSCIENCE

"How much more shall the blood of Christ, who through the eternal Spirit offered Himself without spot to God, cleanse your conscience from dead works to serve the living God." **(Hebrews 9:14)**

GRANTS US ACCESS INTO HIS HOLINESS

"Therefore, brethren, having boldness to enter the Holiest by the blood of Jesus..." **(Hebrews 10:19)**

JUSTIFIES AND SANCTIFIES US

"Much more then, being now justified by his blood, we shall be saved from wrath through him." **Romans 5:9**

"Therefore Jesus also, that He might sanctify the people with His own blood, suffered outside the gate." **(Hebrews 13:12)**

CLEANS US FROM SIN

"But if we walk in the light as He is in the light, we have fellowship with one another, and the blood of Jesus Christ His Son cleanses us from all sin." **(1 John 1:7)**

HEALS US

"Who his own self bare our sins in his own body on the tree, that we, being dead to sins, should live unto righteousness: by whose stripes ye were healed." **1Peter 2:24**

> *"But he was wounded for our transgressions, he was bruised for our iniquities: the chastisement of our peace was upon him; and with his stripes we are healed."*
> **Isaiah 53:5.**

We must take advantage of the blood of Jesus Christ. I encourage you to use the blood of Jesus as a ritual every time you engage in warfare prayer. The blood sanctifies, the blood justifies, and the blood cleanses us from sin and unrighteousness.

Engage the blood of Jesus Christ and be free from all the wiles and schemes of the devil.

CHAPTER 2
The Testimonial Power in the blood of Jesus

"And they overcame him by the blood of the Lamb, and by the word of their testimony; and they loved not their lives unto the death." **Rev 12:11**

The fact that Jesus died and rose from the dead is the everlasting testimony that will never fade.

"And he is the head of the body, the church: who is the beginning, the firstborn from the dead; that in all things he might have the preeminence." **Col 1:18**

"And, having made peace through the blood of his cross, by him to reconcile all things unto himself; by him, I say, whether they be things in earth, or things in heaven." **Col 1:20**

If you have never experienced the testimonial power in the blood of Jesus Christ. I encourage you to say these pray below aloud.

I cover my life with the blood of Jesus.

I cover my family with the blood of Jesus.

I cover my job with the blood of Jesus.

I plead the Blood of Jesus for my healing.

I resist you devil with the Blood of the Lamb.

I plead the blood of Jesus over my business and education.

I plead the blood of Jesus over my wife/husband.

I plead the Blood of the Lord Jesus Christ against this problem.

Chapter 2 - The Testimonial Power in the Blood of Jesus

THE BENEFIT OF THE BLOOD OF JESUS CHRIST

Guaranteed protection:

If you can plead the blood of Jesus Christ in faith, your protection is guaranteed. We were told For he shall give his angels charge over thee, to keep thee in all thy ways.

Unlimited insight:

If you can plead the blood of Jesus in faith and be in the spirit, you will definitely hear from God. Unlimited insight is guaranteed every time we plead the blood of Jesus Christ aright. The word says Deep calleth unto deep at the noise of thy waterspouts: all thy waves and thy billows are gone over me. Apostle John said I was in the Spirit on the Lord's day, and heard behind me a great voice, as of a trumpet,

Protection from sickness and diseases

"That it might be fulfilled which was spoken by Esaias the prophet, saying, Himself took our infirmities, and bare our sicknesses."

If he took away our sickness and disease then we must hold on to that confession and plead the blood of Jesus Christ as often as possible.

"But he was wounded for our transgressions, he was bruised for our iniquities: the chastisement of our peace was upon him; and with his stripes we are healed." **Isaiah53:5**

Un-Stoppable Progress in Life:

We become unstoppable in life, every time we are consistent in prayers that plead the blood of Jesus always. But the path of the just is as the shining light, that shineth more and more unto the perfect day. Proverb4:18.

Victory over life circumstances and challenges.

If you can pray aright, take the necessary action plan required for your next level, you shall surely be victorious.

"For whatsoever is born of God overcometh the world: and this is the victory that overcometh the world, even our faith. Who is he that overcometh the world, but he that believeth that Jesus is the Son of God?" **1John5:4-5**

Released from the curse of the law

The blood of Jesus Christ sets us free from the curse of the law. *"Christ hath redeemed us from the curse of the law, being made a curse for us: for it is written, Cursed is every one that hangeth on a tree:That the blessing of Abraham might come on the Gentiles through Jesus Christ; that we might receive the promise of the Spirit through faith."* **Gal3:13-14**

Cleansing from unrighteousness and Sin:

"But if we walk in the light, as he is in the light, we have fellowship one with another, and the blood of Jesus Christ his Son cleanseth us from all sin. If we say that we have no sin, we deceive ourselves, and the truth is not in us. If we confess our sins, he is faithful and just to forgive us our sins, and to cleanse us from all unrighteousness." **1John1:7-9**

Guaranteed Prosperity:

If you do not plead the blood of Jesus Christ the enemy will continue to attack your finances. You can be prosperous, but with must struggle and sorrows. *"The blessing of the Lord, it maketh rich, and he addeth no sorrow with it."* **Proverb10:22**

WHAT MUST I DO TO PLEAD THE BLOOD OF JESUS CHRIST

1. We must have fellowship and relationship with the Holy Spirit. We must also know all the Bible says about the power of the blood. We must repent of our sins, and confess the Lord Jesus as savior.

2. We must have faith in the power of the blood. For the blood without the shedding of the blood, there is no remission of sin.

3. Apply the blood. Old Testament teaches – The Blood was applied by sprinkling.

New Testament teaches – The Blood is applied by speaking, declaring, prayer.

CONCLUSION

"And almost all things are by the law purged with blood; and without shedding of blood is no remission." **Hebrews9:22**

If we have not been giving thanks even in our prayers. we have not been living right. Thanksgiving must become a daily ritual for every believer.

"Therefore if any man be in Christ, he is a new creature: old things are passed away; behold, all things are become new." **2cor5:17**

Now repeat this Prayer after me

Say Lord Jesus, I accept you today, as my Lord and my savior, forgive me of my sins wash me with your blood. Right now, I believe, I am sanctified, I am save, I am free, I am free from the Power of sin to serve the Lord Jesus. Thank you Lord for saving me. Amen.

What must I do to determine my divine visitation?

To determine divine visitation you must be born again. The word says as many as received him, to them gave He power to become the sons of God. Even to them that believe on his name.

To qualify for divine visitation do the following sincerely;

1) Acknowledge that you are a sinner and that He died for you. **Rom3:23**.

2) Repent of your sins. **Acts 3:19, Luke13:5, 2Peter3:9**

3) Believe in your heart that Jesus died for your sin. **Romans10:10**

4) Confess Jesus as the Lord over your life. **Romans10:10, Acts2:21**

Now repeat this Prayer after me

Say Lord Jesus, I accept you today, as my Lord and my savior, forgive me of my sins wash me with your blood. Right now, I believe, I am sanctified, I am save, I am free, I am free from the Power of sin to serve the Lord Jesus. Thank you Lord for saving me.

Chapter 2 - The Testimonial Power in the Blood of Jesus

I adjure you to watch the Spirit of God bear witness with your Spirit confirming His word with signs following. The word says The Spirit itself beareth witness with our spirit, that we are the children of God.

Join a bible believing church or join us on our weekly and Sunday worship services at 343 Sanford Avenue Newark New Jersey 07106.

WISDOM KEYS

Every Productive Society is a society heading to the top

Millions of Nigerians run away from Nigeria, very few Nigerians stay in Nigeria.

My decision to return Nigeria is the will of God for my life

My short coming in America after 18 years, trained me to be wise, to think, reflect and reason appropriately.

If you train your mind to reason it will train your hands to earn money.

It is absurd to use the money of the heathen to build the kingdom of the living God.

Every Ministry reveals its agenda and goal either at the beginning or at the end. Be careful of your life it is your first Ministry.

The average American mind is conditioned for a continual quest to get new things and (discard the former) and throw away old things.

Chapter 2 - The Testimonial Power in the Blood of Jesus

When I considered well, my BMW jeep became my initial deposit for the work of the ministry in Nigeria

Everyone is waiting for you to change your mind until you change your thinking nothing changes around you.

Multiple academic degrees in other discipline gave me the chance to think, reflect and reason

What so everyone are thinking and reflecting at the moment reveals you to the time and the now factor

All events and intents are the product of precise thought processes, accurate reason every event is designed for a designated timeline

Wisdom is your ability to think, to create and invent. If you can think wise enough you will come out of penury

The distance between you and success is your creative ability to think reason and reflect accurate.

Success is the result of hard work, commitment resolve and determination learning from past mistakes and failing.

If you organize your mind you have organized your life and destiny.

There is a thin line between success and failure. If you look above and beyond you are on your way to success.

Wealth is your ability to think, power is your ability to reason and success is your ability to be informed.

If you can make use of your mind by thinking and reasoning God will make use of your life and destiny.

Think and Be Great

Reflect, Reason, think and be great

Famous people are born of woman

Chapter 2 - The Testimonial Power in the Blood of Jesus

That you will make it is your intention; that you will survive is your resolve, that you will succeed with changes is your determination, personal efforts and hard work.

No man was born a failure. Lack of vision is the end product of failure.

Working with mental patients encourages and aspire me to be a productive observant and dedicated to my assignment.

Successful people are not magicians, it is the will power combined with hard work, and determination and a resolve to succeed that make them succeed.

In the unequivocal state of the mind, intention is not a location or a position it is the state of the mind.

So many people think that they think. The mind is used to think reflect and reason. You will remain blind with your eye open until you can see with your mind by thinking.

There is no favoritism in accurate and precise calculation

Although knowledge is power, information is the key and gateway to a great future.

It will take the hand of God to move the hand of man.

With the backing of the great wise God, nothing will disconnect you from your inheritance.

As long as you have wisdom and understanding of God, Satan and evil cannot manipulate your life and destiny.

You have come this far by yourself judgment and decision you have made in the past, now lean and listen to God for another dimension of greatness.

Great people are common people it is extra ordinary effort and the price of sacrifice that produces greatness.

As a mental direct care worker I saw a great pastor and a motivational speaker within myself.

Menial job does not reduce your self-worth, until you resolve to achieve greatness see greatness in all you do; you will never count in your community

hapter 2 - The Testimonial Power in the Blood of Jesus

The principle of Jesus will solve your gambling and addiction problems

The man of Jesus will lead you into heaven,

Everyone have their self-appraisal and what they think about you. Until you discover yourself other opinion about you will alter the real you.

Supervisors and directors are just a position in the chain of command in a work place. Never allow your supervisor hierarchy to alter your opinion about yourself.

Everyone can come out of debt if they make up their mind.

That I am not a decision maker at work does not diminish my contribution to my world.

Although it appears like it was a poor decision to accept a direct care employment at a psychiatric hospital as I reflect of my nine years of experience, it became apparent that I have learnt and experienced enough for my next assignment.

Self-encouragement and determination is a resolve of the heart.

If you are determined to make a difference, and do the things that make a difference you will eventually make a difference.

Good things do not come easy

Short cuts will cut your life short.

Those who look ahead move ahead.

Life is all about making an impact. In your life time strive to make an impact in your community.

Make friends and connect with people who are moving ahead of you in life.

If you can look around well you have come a long way in your life, made a lot of difference and realized a lot of success in life.

If you are my old friend, hurry up to reach out to me before I become a stranger to you.

Everything I am blessed with inspirations from God, that change my definition and interpretation of the world around me.

I thought I was stagnant and lonely until I looked around and noticed my children running around and my wife cooking.

Chapter 2 - The Testimonial Power in the Blood of Jesus

At 40 I resigned my Job to seek the Lord forever.

My ministry took a drastic rise to the top when the wisdom of God visited me with knowledge and understanding.

You will be a better person if you understand the characteristics of your personality – your mood swings attitudes and habits.

It is the seed of love you sow into the heart of a child and a woman that you reap in due time.

Love is not selfish, love share everything including the concealed secrets of the mind.

As long as you have a prayer life and a bible; you will never feel lonely, rejected and idle in the race of life.

When good friends disconnect from you, let them go, they might have seen something new in a different direction.

Confidence in yourself and in God is the only way to bring you out of captivity

Never train a child to waste his/her time.

The mind is the greatest assets of a great future.

You walk by common sense run by principles and fly by instruction.

Those who fly in flight of life fly alone.

Up in the air you are alone. No one can toll you accept the compass of knowledge and information

I have seen a tolling vehicle I have seen a tolling ship I have never seen a tolling airplane.

I exercise my judgment and make a decision every minute of the day.

Decisions are crucial, critical and vital with reference to your future.

So many people wish for a great future. You can only work towards a great future.

Your celebrity status began when you discovered your talent. What are you good at? Work at it with all commitment.

Prayers will sustain you but the wisdom of God will prosper you.

When I met Oyedepo, his teachings changed my perspective, but when I met Ibiyeomie; His teaching changed my perception.

Chapter 2 - The Testimonial Power in the Blood of Jesus

I will be successful in ministry if only I concentrate and focus my energy in the work of the ministry.

It took the late Dr. Vincent Pearle Norman's book to open my mind towards kingdom success.

CHAPTER 3
PRAYER OF SALVATION

"Neither is there salvation in any other: for there is none other name under heaven given among men, whereby we must be saved." **Acts4:12**

One of the reasons we suffer bitterness, hatred and rejection is because we do not know the power in the Name of Jesus. I want you to consciously take the Name of Jesus serious in your life. Believe in that name. It will deliver you from relationship nightmares, and bitterness.

The word of God says *"The name of the Lord is a strong tower: the righteous runneth into it, and is safe."* **Proverb18:10**

Are you saved?

To be saved we must be born again!

The word says as many as received him, to them gave He power to become the sons of God. Even to them that believe on his name.

To qualify for divine visitation do the following sincerely,

1) Acknowledge that you are a sinner and that He died for you. **Rom3:23.**

2) Repent of your sins. **Acts 3:19, Luke13:5, 2Peter3:9**

3) Believe in your heart that Jesus died for your sin. **Romans10:10**

4) Confess Jesus as the Lord over your life. **Romans10:10, Acts2:21**

Now repeat this Prayer after me

Say Lord Jesus, I accept you today, as my Lord and my savior, forgive me of my sins wash me with your blood. Right now, I believe, I am sanctified, I am save, I am free, I am free from the Power of sin to serve the Lord Jesus. Thank you Lord for saving me. Amen.

Join a bible believing church or you can join us proclaim the power of God in the gospel of Jesus Christ. There is Power in the blood of the lamb.

Chapter 3 - Prayer of Salvation

MIRACLE CARE OUTREACH

"...But that the members should have the same care one for another" **1cor12:25**

We are all members of the body of Christ. Jesus commanded us to love our neighbor as ourselves. This includes caring for one another as a member of one body. True love is expressed in caring and giving. The word says for God so Love He gave….

Reach out to someone in need of Jesus, help someone in crisis find Christ. Look out and prove your love to Jesus by caring and inviting your friends and associates to find Jesus the Healer.

Invite your friends to our Home Care Cell Fellowship (Miracle chapel Intl Satellite fellowship) In the USA at 33 Schley Street Newark New Jersey 07112.

If you are in Nigeria—**MIRACLE OF GOD MINISTRIES**

**A.K.A"MIRACLE CHAPEL INTL"
Mpama –Egbu-Owerri Imo state Nigeria.**

(Home Care Cell fellowship Group). We meet every Tuesday at 6:00pm-7:00pm.

LIFE IS NOT ALL ABOUT DURATION BUT ITS ALL ABOUT DONATION

What does the above statement mean?....

"Life consists not in accumulation of material wealth.." **Luke12:15.**

"But it's all about liberality....meaning- what you can give and share with others." **Proverb11:25.**

When you live for others--You live forever- because you out live your generation by the legacy you live behind after you depart into glory to be with the Lord. But when you live to yourself - you are reduced to self—you are easily forgotten when you die and depart in glory.

Permit me to admonish you today to live your life to be a blessing to a soul connected to you today.

Chapter 3 - Prayer of Salvation

I want you to know that so many souls are connected and looking up to you, and through you so many souls will be saved and rescued from destruction. Will you disciple someone today to find Jesus Christ?

"As a genuine Christian; it is your duty to evangelize Jesus Christ to all you meet on your way. Jesus is still in the healing business-Jesus is still doing miracles from time of old to now.

Therefore tell someone about Jesus Christ today, disciple and bring them to Church."

John 1:45 Philip findeth Nathanael....

Please to prove the sincerity of your love for God today; please become a soul winner. The dignity of your Christianity is hidden in your boldness to proclaim and evangelize Jesus Christ to all you meet on your way.

There is a question mark on the integrity of your Christianity until you become a life soul winner. Invite someone to join us worship the Lord Jesus this coming Sunday.

MIRACLE OF GOD MINISTRIES

PILLARS OF THE COMMISSION

We Believe Preach and Practice the following,

1) We believe and preach Salvation to every living human being

2) We believe and preach Repentance and forgiveness of sins

3) We believe and preach the baptism of the Holy Spirit and Spiritual gifts

4) We believe and teach the Prosperity

5) We believe and preach Divine Healing and Miracles (Signs & Wonder)

6) We believe and preach Faith

7) We believe and Proclaim the Power of God (Supernatural)

8) We believe and Proclaim Praise & Worship to God

Chapter 3 - Prayer of Salvation

9) We believe and preach Wisdom

10) We believe and preach Holiness (Consecration)

11) We believe and preach Vision

12) We believe and teach the Word of God

13) We believe and teach Success

14) We believe and practice Prayer

15) We believe and teach Deliverance

This 15 stones form the Pillars of Our Commission.

Become part of this church family and follow this great move of God.

MY HEART FELT PRAYER FOR YOU

It is my prayer that you testify today about the goodness of the Lord. I desire for you to overcome the memory of any divorce if any in your life in the mighty name of Jesus Christ.

Now let me Pray for you:

Heavenly father may today be a day of new beginning for this precious love one. Lord God of heaven open a new chapter in the life of this precious love one reading this book today. May all their prayers be answered in the mighty name of Jesus. We thank you Jesus for hearing us. In Jesus mighty name.

Amen.

Chapter 3 - Prayer of Salvation

Encounter with God

Unless you are left alone you are not ready to encounter God. Jacob was left alone and he encountered God. I strongly urge you to create a quiet time with your God. A time of meditation and reflection. God is still omnipotent and all powerful. But you have to discover this by prayer and meditation in the word of God.

Jacob encountered God

"And Jacob was left alone; and there wrestled a man with him until the breaking of the day. And when he saw that he prevailed not against him, he touched the hollow of his thigh; and the hollow of Jacob's thigh was out of joint, as he wrestled with him. And he said, Let me go, for the day breaketh. And he said, I will not let thee go, except thou bless me. And he said unto him, What is thy name? And he said, Jacob. And he said, Thy name shall be called no more Jacob, but Israel: for as a prince hast thou power with God and with men, and hast prevailed." **Genesis 32:24-28**.

Apostle Paul encountered God

"And as he journeyed, he came near Damascus: and suddenly there shined round about him a light from heaven: And he fell to the earth, and heard a voice saying unto him, Saul, Saul, why persecutest thou me? And he said, Who art thou, Lord? And the Lord said, I am Jesus whom thou persecutest: it is hard for thee to kick against the pricks." **Acts9:3-5**

CHAPTER 4
ABOUT THE AUTHOR

Rev Franklin N Abazie is the founding and Presiding Pastor of Miracle of God Ministries with headquarters in Newark, New Jersey USA and a branch church in Owerri- Imo State Nigeria. He is following the footsteps of one of his mentors, Oral Roberts (Healing Evangelist) of the blessed memory.

The Lord passed Oral Roberts healing mantle two days before he went to be with the Lord at age 91 into the hand of healing evangelist-Rev Franklin N Abazie in a vision.

In all his services the Power and Presence of God is present to heal all in his audience. He is an ordained man of God with a Healing Ministry reviving the healing and miracle ministry of Jesus Christ of Nazareth.

Pastor Franklin N Abazie, is called by God with a unique mandate:

"THE MOMENT IS DUE TO IMPACT YOUR WORLD THROUGH THE REVIVAL OF THE HEALING & MIRACLE MINISTRY OF JESUS CHRIST OF NAZARETH.

I AM SENDING YOU TO RESTORE HEALTH UNTO THEE AND I WILL HEAL THEE OF THY WOUNDS. SAID THE LORD OF HOST"

He is a gifted ardent Teacher of the word of God who operates also in the office of a Prophet, generating and attracting undeniable signs & wonders, special miracles and healings, with apostolic fireworks of the Holy Ghost.

He is the founding and presiding senior Pastor of this fast growing Healing ministry.

He has written over 86 inspirational, healing and transforming books covering almost all aspect of divine healing and life. He is happily married and blessed with children.

BOOKS BY REV FRANKLIN N ABAZIE

1) Commanding Abundance
2) The outcome of faith
3) Understanding the secret of prevailing prayers
4) Understanding the secret of the man God uses
5) Activating my due Season
6) Overcoming Divine Verdicts
7) The Outcome of Divine Wisdom
8) Understanding God's Restoration Mandate
9) Walking in the Victory and Authority of the truth
10) Gods Covenant Exemption
11) Destiny Restoration Pillars
12) Provoking Acceptable Praise
13) Understanding Divine Judgment
14) Activating Angelic Re-enforcement
15) Provoking Un-Merited Favor
16) The Benefits of the Speaking faith
17) Understanding Divine Arrangement

18) Understanding Divine Healing
19) The Mystery of Endurance
20) Obeying Divine Instructions
21) Understanding the Voice of God
22) Never give up on Hope
23) The prevailing Power of faith
24) Understanding Divine Prosperity
25) The Reward of Prayer
26) Covenant Keys to Answered Prayers
27) Activating the Forces of Vengeance
28) Put your faith to work
29) Where is your trust?
30) The Audacity of the Blood of Jesus
31) Redeeming Your Days
32) The force of Vision
33) Breaking the shackles of Family Curses
34) Wisdom for Marriage Stability
35) Overcoming prevailing challenges
36) The Prayer solution
37) The power of Prayer
38) The Effective Strategy of Prayer
39) The prayer that works
40) Walking in Forgiveness
41) The power of the grace of God

42) The Power of Persistence
43) Overcoming Divine verdicts
44) The audacity of the blood of Jesus.
45) The prevailing power of the blood of Jesus
46) The benefit of the speaking faith.
47) Fearless faith
48) Redeeming Your Days.
49) The Supernatural Power of Prophecy
50) The companionship of the Holy Spirit
51) Understanding Divine Judgement
52) Understanding Divine Prosperity
53) Dominating Controlling Forces
54) The winners Faith
55) Destiny Restoration Pillars
56) Developing Spiritual Muscles
57) Inexplicable faith
58) The lifestyle of Prayer
59) Developing a positive attitude in life.
60) The mystery of Divine supply
61) Encounter with the Power of God
62) Walking in love
63) Praying in the Spirit
64) How to provoke your testimony

65) Walking in the reality of the Anointing
66) The reality of new birth
67) The price of freedom
68) The Supernatural power of faith
69) The intellectual components of Redemption
70) Overcoming Fear
71) Overcoming Prevailing Challenges
72) My life & Ministry
73) The Mystery of Praise

MIRACLE OF GOD MINISTRIES
NIGERIA CRUSADE 2012

MIRACLE OF GOD MINISTRIES
NIGERIA CRUSADE 2012

MIRACLE OF GOD MINISTRIE

NIGERIA CRUSADE

2012

**MIRACLE
OF
GOD
MINISTRIES**

NIGERIA CRUSADE

2012

www.ingramcontent.com/pod-product-compliance
Lightning Source LLC
Chambersburg PA
CBHW021133300426
44113CB00006B/407